In loving memory of Ais
Dedicated to the star po

BE HUMBLE FOR YOU ARE MADE OF EARTH.

BE NOBLE FOR YOU ARE MADE OF STARS.

—SERBIAN PROVERB

Minneapolis, MN 55455
www.leadtolove.com

All rights reserved. Published by Lead to Love Publishing.

ISBN-13: 978-1503200920
ISBN-10: 1503200922

Library of Congress Control Number: 2015919688

"Success means we go to sleep at night knowing that our talents and abilities were used in a way that served others."
— Marianne Williamson

YOU ARE MADE OF
— STARS —

Why life and leadership are about shining your light

KRISTI L. KREMERS

On one special starry night,
Mommy and Daddy wished
with all their might,
and a sweet song leapt into
their hearts.

They taught this song to the doctor and nurses, to your grandparents, and then you arrived.

We welcomed you into this world by singing your song:

"You are made of stars.

Your greatest gift is your sparkle.

Shine bright, oh precious one,
for life and leadership
are always about shining your
light!"

We'll sing your song in happy times.

And we'll sing your song in dark times too.

If you ever get lost and make a misstep, we'll circle around you and sing you your song to remind you of who you truly are.

For you are made of stars, my dear, and what a star you are!

As you find your way
through this world, sweet
child, remember what
Grandma taught you about
the great Sufi way.

The old Sufis taught that our words had to pass through three golden gates:

The first gate asked, "Is it true?"

The second gate asked, "Is it necessary?"

Finally, the third gate asked, "Is it kind?"

It is better to be silent than to speak words that do not pass through these three gates.

14

There are so many ways to shine your light and set your spirit free!

Kindness is one of the ways to sparkle. Razzle and dazzle and be the best that you can be.

You can be front and center and lead the song, or be a backup dancer and dance along.

Or, as the Sufis say, sometimes it is best to be silent, singing your song this way.

Discover your own
genius, my sweet child.

And in this space you'll find,
when you know and own
your star power,
life is limitless and sublime!

There is one thing I hope
you will call to mind no
matter where life takes you:
In highs and lows,
thunderclouds and sunshine,
it is best to be kind
whenever possible,
and it is always possible to be
kind.

For you are made of stars,
and someday,
you will find a way to help
others feel and know that
they are made of stars too.

There are so many things I wish
for you to know sweetheart.
For there will come a time,
when day turns into night...
when you will need to sing me
my song,
as I take flight.

When you miss me,
wrap your arms around the ones
you love,
and look up into the starry sky
above.

See the star that winks and
twinkles?

That's me singing my song back
to you.

For you are made of stars my
dear, and I am too.

Activities & Discussion Guides

"The nitrogen in our DNA, the calcium in our teeth, the iron in our blood, the carbon in our apple pies were made in the interiors of collapsing stars.

We are made of star-stuff."

-

Carl Sagan

You Are Made of Stars

Our bodies are made of molecules and atoms from exploding stars.
* About 93% of our body mass is made of stardust.
* Every element on the periodic table
except for hydrogen comes from stardust.

For more resources on the science of the stars, visit: www.leadtolove.com

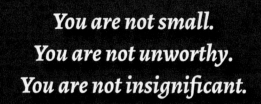

You are not small.
You are not unworthy.
You are not insignificant.

The universe wove you from a constellation...
every fiber in you comes from a different star.

Together, you are bound by stardust, altogether spectacularly created from the energy of the universe itself.

And that, my darling, is the poetry of physics, the poetry of you.

~Nikita Gill

For discussion:
What does this poem mean to you?

Leader Profiles

> Be kind whenever possible.
>
> It is always possible.

> My legacy is that I stayed on course...from the beginning to the end, because I believed in something inside of me.

> I don't think of work as work and play as play.
>
> It's all living.

The Dalai Lama

The Dalai Lama is a Buddhist monk and world leader. He believes that compassion is the key to a happy life.

Questions for Discussion:
What is compassion? Is it always possible to be kind? Why or why not? How can you be compassionate today?

Tina Turner

Tina Turner is an author, dancer, actress and one of the best-selling recording artists of all-time. Her life story included many highs and lows.

Questions for Discussion:
What is the meaning of "staying the course"? Why is this important in life and leadership?

Richard Branson

Richard Branson is an adventurer, businessman and investor who oversees over 400 companies.

Questions for Discussion:
Describe how you feel when you play. Can you imagine a career where work would feel like playtime?

ALBERT EINSTEIN

Scientist, leader and daydreamer

Born in Germany, Albert Einstein is perhaps the most famous scientist of our time. At the age of five, his father gave him a compass which helped inspire his love for science at an early age.

Einstein developed his most important theories and ideas through daydreams.

Questions for discussion:
What makes a great daydream? How are daydreams powerful tools that a leader can use to solve problems?

THE TRUE SIGN OF INTELLIGENCE IS NOT KNOWLEDGE BUT IMAGINATION.

Albert Einstein

SHINE YOUR LIGHT

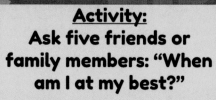

Activity:
Ask five friends or family members: "When am I at my best?"

Discussion Guide
for families

1. As a family, how do we recognize and celebrate the star power in one another?

2. What traditions, from our ancestors, honor the star power within us? What new traditions can we create?

3. If a family member does something that does not represent our family values (for example: lie, cheat, or steal), how can we remind them of their star power?

4. How would you like to be reminded of your star power?

ACTIVITY: STAR POWER PARTY
Invite grandparents and close family friends.
Sit in a circle with your favorite people.
Each person will take a turn to sit in the center of the circle.
They cannot speak. They are only there to receive.
Take turns telling them about their star power
and watch how they shine!

"Stop acting so small. You are the universe in ecstatic motion."
~ Rumi

1. In our classroom, how do we recognize and celebrate the star power in one another?

2. How can we make room for those who are shy to let their star power shine?

3. How do we help someone reconnect with their star power when they have forgotten it?

JOURNAL ACTIVITY

Sometimes our star power can be loud and visible. Sometimes it can be hidden and quiet. Make a list of all the ways you activate your star power.

CLASSROOM ACTIVITY

Watch a video to explore the science behind our stardust origins. Search for one that best meets the needs of your class. Here's an example from Carl Sagan: http://tinyurl.com/youaremadeofstars

"It is the supreme art of the teacher to awaken joy in creative expression and knowledge." — *Albert Einstein*

See the Light and Sparkle in Others

Write a letter to someone who inspires you. It could be someone not well-known, a friend, or a family member.

What is their star power? What makes them shine?

KRISTI L. KREMERS has been teaching at colleges and universities for the past decade. Her primary research interests include: emotional intelligence, ethics, neuroleadership, applied mindfulness in leadership, and how organizations can adapt an anthropological approach to creating culture and community. She is also an RYT-500 yoga instructor who has studied extensively in India.

In developing *Lead to Love*, it is her wish to create tools and resources for families and teachers to instill both a love of leadership and a mindset to "lead with love" in children.

Visit Kristi's website: www.kristikremers.com
Author photo by the ultra-talented Tegan Jae: www.teganjae.com

Lead to love

MINDFULNESS & WELL-BEING

SELF-ESTEEM & SELF-KNOWLEDGE

GREAT LEADERSHIP

VALUES & ETHICS

"Teaching kids to count is fine, but teaching them what counts is best."
-Bob Talbert

Made in the USA
Las Vegas, NV
09 January 2025

16094784R00029